The Magic School Bus
Inside the Human Body

By Joanna Cole   Illustrated by Bruce Degen

SCHOLASTIC
HARDCOVER

SCHOLASTIC INC. / *New York*

The author and illustrator wish to thank Dr. Arnold J. Capute,
Associate Professor of Pediatrics, Director, Division of Child Development,
Johns Hopkins University School of Medicine, for his help in preparing this book.

Library of Congress Cataloging-in-Publication Data
Cole, Joanna.
The magic school bus.
Summary: A special field trip on the
magic school bus allows Ms. Frizzle's class to get
a first-hand look at major parts of the
body and how they work.
1. Metabolism—Juvenile literature.   [1. Body, Human]
I. Degen, Bruce, ill.   II. Title.
QP171.C66   1988   612   88-3070
ISBN 0-590-41426-7

12   11   10   3   4/9

Printed in the U.S.A.   36

First Scholastic printing, May 1989

It all began when Ms. Frizzle
showed our class a filmstrip
about the human body.
We knew trouble was about to start,
because we knew Ms. Frizzle
was the strangest teacher in the school.

YOUR BODY IS MADE OF CELLS
by Rachel

Your body seems to be all one piece, but actually it is made of trillions of tiny pieces, called cells.

MY BODY IS MADE OF TRILLIONS OF CELLS.

SO IS MINE!

The very next day, The Friz made us do an experiment on our own bodies.

SEE YOUR OWN CELLS

Most cells are so small that we can't see them without a microscope.

① Gently scrape inside of cheek with toothpick

② Stir end of toothpick in drop of water on a slide.

③ Add a drop of Iodine Solution to color cells.

④ Look at slide under microscope. See your cells.

OOOH, WEIRD!

Then she announced that we were going on a class trip to the science museum. We were going to see an exhibit about how our bodies get energy from the food we eat.

YOUR CELLS NEED ENERGY TO HELP YOU GROW, MOVE, TALK, THINK, AND PLAY.

JUST BEING IN MS. FRIZZLE'S CLASS TAKES ALL MY ENERGY.

DIFFERENT KINDS OF CELLS HAVE DIFFERENT JOBS
by Gregory

Lung cells help you breathe.

Muscle Cells help you move.

Brain Cells help you think.

When it was time to go,
everyone got back on the bus—
everyone but Arnold.
He was still at the picnic table,
daydreaming and eating
a bag of Cheesie-Weesies.

WHEN YOU EAT, YOUR BODY <u>DIGESTS</u> THE FOOD SO YOUR CELLS CAN USE IT TO MAKE ENERGY.

YOUR BODY NEEDS GOOD FOOD
by Carmen
For high energy and good growing power eat lots of:

Fresh fruits and Vegetables

Milk and Milk products

Whole grain cereal and Pasta

Lean Meats, Fish, Poultry, and eggs

AND <u>NOT</u> TOO MUCH JUNK FOOD

A SCIENCE WORD
by Dorothy Ann

<u>Digestion</u> comes from a word that means to divide. When food is digested it is divided into smaller and smaller parts.

"Hurry up, Arnold!" called Ms. Frizzle. She reached for the ignition key, but instead she pushed a strange little button nearby.

ARNOLD'S REALLY OUT TO LUNCH.

At once, we started shrinking and spinning through the air.

From inside, we couldn't see what was happening. All we knew was that we landed suddenly...

GULP! HEY, WHERE'S THE BUS?

CHEESIE WEESIES

EESIE EESIES

and then we were going down a dark tunnel.
We had no idea where we were.
But, as usual, Ms. Frizzle knew.
She said we were inside a human body,
going down the esophagus—
the tube that leads from the throat
to the stomach.
Most of us were too upset
about leaving Arnold behind
to pay much attention.

WHERE'S ARNOLD?

HE GOT LEFT.!

THAT'S WHAT HAPPENS WHEN YOU EAT JUNK FOOD!

I THOUGHT WE WERE GOING TO THE MUSEUM.

THERE'S BEEN A SLIGHT CHANGE OF PLANS... WE'RE BEING DIGESTED INSTEAD.

FOOD GOES TO YOUR STOMACH THROUGH THE ESOPHAGUS
by Wanda
The food does not just fall down. It is pushed along by muscle actions the way toothpaste is squeezed out of a tube. That's why you can swallow even when you are upside down.

MUSCLES SQUEEZE TO PUSH FOOD TO YOUR STOMACH

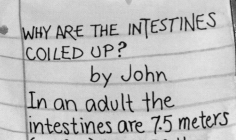

WHY ARE THE INTESTINES COILED UP?
by John
In an adult the intestines are 7.5 meters (25 feet) long. If they were stretched out straight, a person would have to be as tall as a house.

STOMACH

FOOD GOES FROM THE STOMACH TO THE SMALL INTESTINE

WASTE GOES OUT THROUGH THE LARGE INTESTINE

The small intestine was
a coiled-up hollow tube.
The inner walls of the tube were covered
with tiny "fingers" called *villi*.
"In the *villi* are tiny blood vessels.
Food molecules are taken into
these blood vessels,"
said Ms. Frizzle.
"Once the food is in the blood,
it can travel all over the body."

We felt ourselves getting even smaller,
and Ms. Frizzle started driving
into one of the *villi*.
She was going straight into a blood vessel!

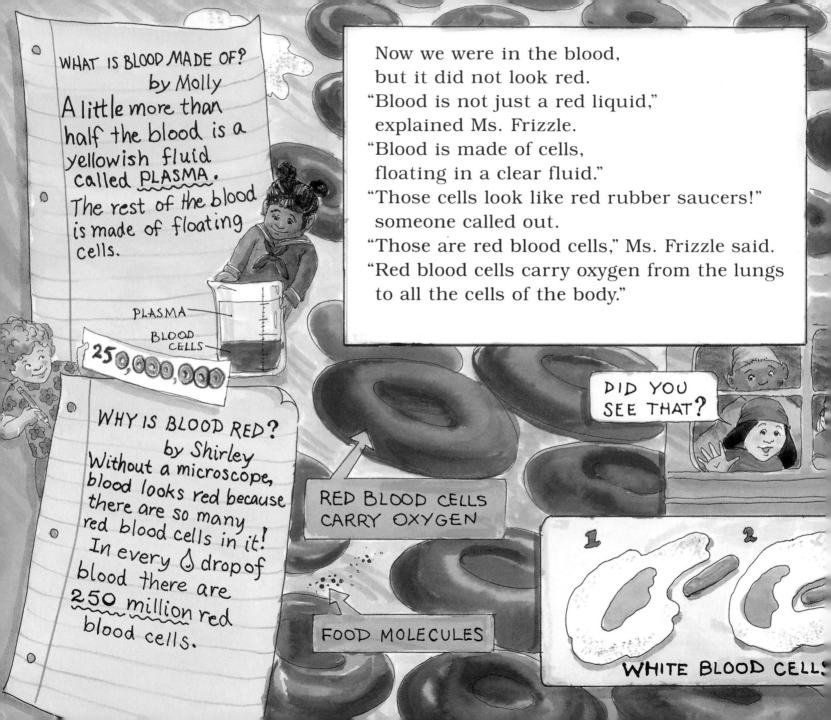

WHAT IS BLOOD MADE OF?
by Molly

A little more than half the blood is a yellowish fluid called PLASMA.
The rest of the blood is made of floating cells.

PLASMA
BLOOD CELLS
250,000,000,000

WHY IS BLOOD RED?
by Shirley

Without a microscope, blood looks red because there are so many red blood cells in it! In every drop of blood there are 250 million red blood cells.

Now we were in the blood,
but it did not look red.
"Blood is not just a red liquid,"
explained Ms. Frizzle.
"Blood is made of cells,
floating in a clear fluid."
"Those cells look like red rubber saucers!"
someone called out.
"Those are red blood cells," Ms. Frizzle said.
"Red blood cells carry oxygen from the lungs
to all the cells of the body."

RED BLOOD CELLS CARRY OXYGEN

DID YOU SEE THAT?

FOOD MOLECULES

1   2

WHITE BLOOD CELLS

Here and there a white blood cell was busy destroying disease germs. "White blood cells are like soldiers protecting your body from enemies," said Ms. Frizzle.

WHAT IS BLOOD FOR?
by Ralph
Your blood is like a delivery service. It carries food and oxygen to your body's cells and waste products away from the cells.

THE WHITE BLOOD CELL ATE THE GERM.

THAT'S DISGUSTING!

PLATELET CELLS
(HELP STOP BLEEDING WHEN YOU GET A CUT)

FOOD

RALPH'S DELIVERY

DESTROY DISEASE GERMS

DISEASE GERMS

Looking back, we saw a white blood cell
chasing the bus.
"We'll be safer with the red blood cells, kids,"
said Ms. Frizzle.
She reached for the handle
that controlled the bus's doors.
"Don't do it!" we cried,
but when did Ms. Frizzle ever listen?
The doors of the bus flew open.

THAT WHITE BLOOD
CELL MUST THINK
THE SCHOOL BUS
IS A GERM.

WELL, THE BUS
IS PRETTY DIRTY.

BLOOD GOES ROUND
AND ROUND
        by Michael
In less than a minute
your blood makes
a trip all around
your body.
    This is called the
circulation of the
blood.

ONE MORE SCIENCE WORD
        by Dorothy Ann
Circulate comes from
a word that means
"to circle". Blood
Circulates - circles -
all around your body.

From the lungs, our red blood cells
carried us back to the heart.
This time we were on the left side
of the heart—the side that pumps
fresh blood back to the body again.
"Kids, it looks as if these red
blood cells are on their way to
the brain," said Ms. Frizzle.

LOOK! WHEN THE
RED BLOOD CELLS
PICK UP OXYGEN, THEY
TURN BRIGHT RED.

FROM RIGHT LUN

AIR
SAC

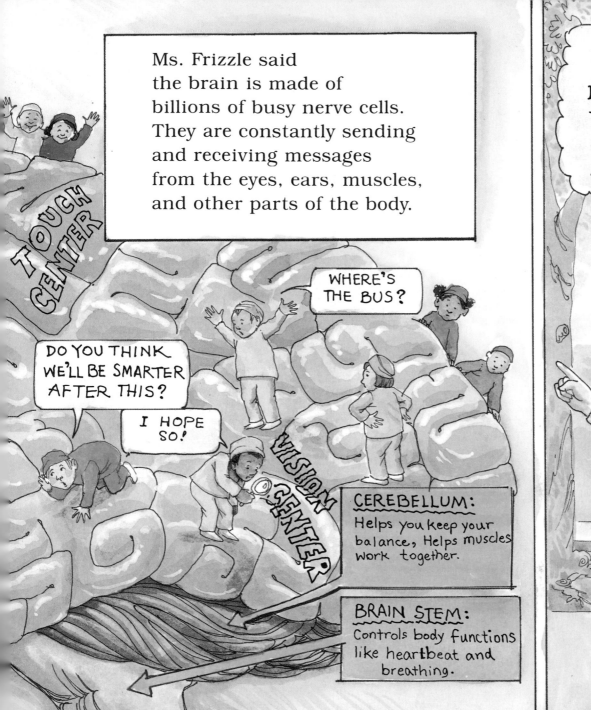

Ms. Frizzle said the brain is made of billions of busy nerve cells. They are constantly sending and receiving messages from the eyes, ears, muscles, and other parts of the body.

TOUCH CENTER

WHERE'S THE BUS?

DO YOU THINK WE'LL BE SMARTER AFTER THIS?

I HOPE SO!

VISION CENTER

CEREBELLUM: Helps you keep your balance. Helps muscles work together.

BRAIN STEM: Controls body functions like heartbeat and breathing.

LET'S SEE... MS. FRIZZLE WAS DRIVING THAT WAY TO THE MUSEUM, SO OUR SCHOOL MUST BE THIS WAY.

GOOD THINKING.

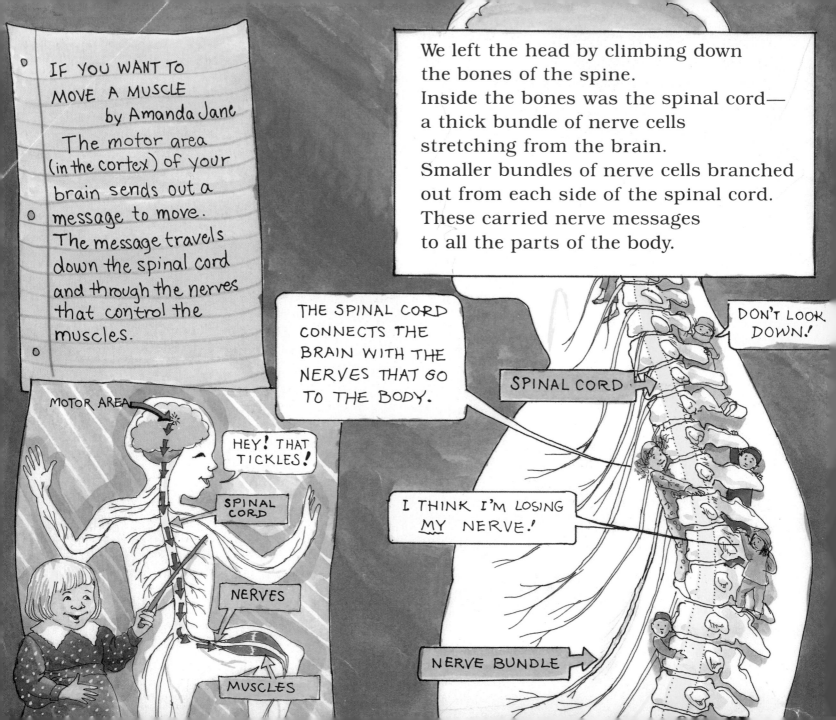

We followed some nerves that went to the leg muscles.
The leg muscles were working hard.
They needed a lot of energy.
They used up a lot of food and oxygen from the blood.
The heart was beating faster to carry fresh blood to the muscle cells.

We entered a nearby blood vessel.
The blood was moving so fast,
we were afraid we would
lose each other.
But at that moment,
the school bus floated by.
What a relief!
We jumped on and went up
through the heart and lungs again—
just the way we went before.

CLASS, WE'RE ON THE WAY OUT OF THE BODY.

RELAX, WE'RE GOING BACK NOW.

I CAN'T RELAX AS LONG AS I SEE BLOOD CELLS OUTSIDE THE WINDOW.

When we emerged from the bloodsteam,
we were in a huge open space.
"Where are we?" asked a kid.
Ms. Frizzle explained,
"Children, this is the nasal cavity."
"The what?" we asked.
"The inside of the nose," said The Friz.
Suddenly, we heard a deafening noise.
It sounded like "Ah-aa-aa-ah!"

WE'RE IN A NOSE?

I AM SO GROSSED OUT!

THIS TIME SHE'S GONE TOO FAR.

I THINK I'M GOING TO SNEEZE...

USE YOUR HANKIE.

WHAT MAKES YOU SNEEZE?
by Phoebe
If something is tickling the inside of your nose, the tickling signals your brain.
The brain makes you take an extra big breath. (That's when you say Aaah!)
Then your brain makes your chest muscles squeeze your lungs.
Air rushes out at speeds of up to 100 miles per hour. (Thats when you say choo!)
Then we heard, "CHOOOOOO!"
CLASS, THE SOUND YOU HEAR IS A SNEEZE.
ANYTHING IN THE NOSE CAN MAKE YOU SNEEZE. IT COULD BE A BIT OF DIRT OR DUST, OR SOME BACTERIA.
IN THIS CASE IT HAPPENS TO BE A SCHOOL BUS.

A tremendous blast of air
hit the bus full force.
We flew forward,
spinning around and around.

We were going so fast,
we couldn't see anything,
but we could tell we were getting bigger.
Then—thud!—we landed.
There we were, back at school.
And there was Arnold,
in the school parking lot,
blowing his nose.

WE'RE BACK!

LOOK! THERE'S ARNOLD!

THUD

"Arnold!" we said, "the trip was *amazing!*
You should have been there!"

WHERE WERE YOU?

Back in the classroom, it was business as usual. Ms. Frizzle made us draw a chart of the human body for the bulletin board.

THE KIDNEYS CLEAN YOUR BLOOD AND MAKE URINE.

THE BLADDER STORES URINE.

KIDNEYS

BLADDER

LIVER

STOMACH

THE LIVER STORES VITAMINS AND DESTROYS POISONS. IT ALSO MAKES BILE, A FLUID THAT HELPS DIGEST FATTY FOODS.

NERVE

BLOOD VESSEL

BONE

MUSCLE

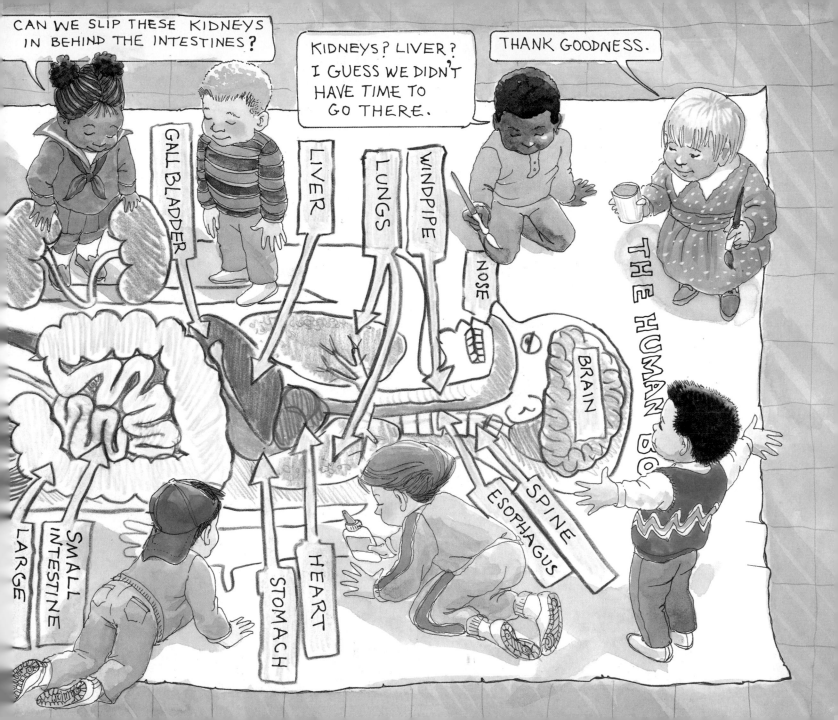

TRUE-OR-FALSE TEST

STOP! TAKE THIS TEST!
DO NOT WATCH T.V. ... YET.
DO NOT GET A SNACK...YET.
DO NOT PLAY A VIDEO
GAME ... YET.

FIRST TAKE THIS TEST.

HOW TO:
Read the sentences below. Decide if each one is true or false. To see if you are correct, check the answers on the opposite page.

QUESTIONS:

1. A school bus can enter someone's body and kids can go on a tour. True or false?

2. Museums are boring. True or false?

3. Arnold should not have tried to get back to school by himself. True or false?

4. Children cannot breathe or talk when they are surrounded by a liquid. True or false?

5. If the children really were as small as cells, we couldn't see them without a microscope. True or false?

6. White blood cells actually chase and destroy disease germs. True or false?

7. Ms. Frizzle really knew where Arnold was the whole time. True or false?

ANSWERS:

1. False! That could not happen in real life. (Not even to Arnold.)

   But in this story the author had to make it happen. Otherwise, the book would have been about a trip to a museum, instead of a trip through the body.

2. False! Museums are interesting and fun. But they are not as weird and gross as actually going inside a human body.

3. True! In real life, it would have been safer if Arnold had found a police officer to help.

4. True. If children were *really* inside a blood vessel, they would drown. It must have been magic.

5. True! The pictures in this book show the cells and the children greatly enlarged.

6. True! As unbelievable as it seems, real white blood cells actually behave just like the ones in this book. They even squeeze through the cells of blood vessel walls to capture germs in your organs and tissues.

7. Probably true. No one is absolutely sure, but most people think Ms. Frizzle knows *everything.*

PLEASE DO NOT WRITE IN THIS BOOK.

THANK YOU.